Top Gun Management

Top Gun Management

Principles for Success and Supremacy

By Gene McVay

Edited by

Marcene Renee McVay, M.D., B.S. Ch. E.

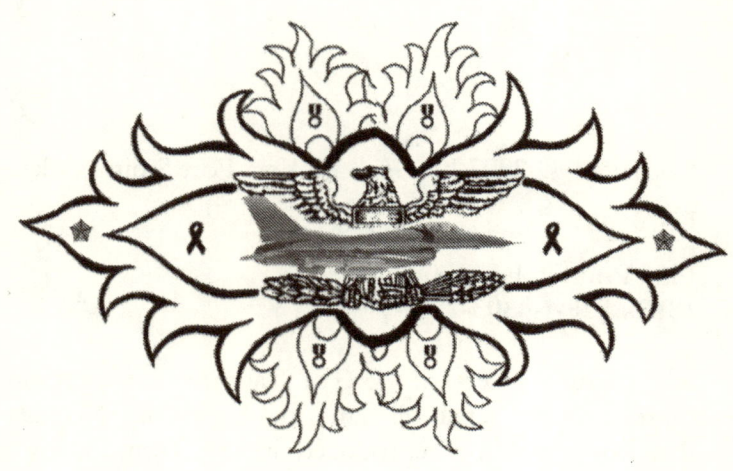

This book is dedicated to the men and women who have donned the uniforms of the United States Armed Forces and served courageously where our country has sent them.

Second Lieutenant McVay preparing to mount the supersonic T-38 Talon for his first solo flight in 1968 at Vance Air Force Base, Oklahoma.

Contents

Introduction

Top Gun CEO's, managers and executives are not unlike fighter pilots who fly 700 miles-per-hour and one hundred feet off the ground on the way to a target in enemy territory. The fighter pilot is focused, prepared, indomitable and determined to complete the mission. While every inch a professional who makes the complex seem routine, the combat pilot is never complacent. Radar guided anti-aircraft artillery and surface-to-air missiles have a way of curtailing the romance of being a fighter pilot. Any enemy who would dare to acquire one of my fighters on radar would not long survive. Such contingencies are contemplated during the planning phase while sophisticated onboard warning systems give pilots detailed indications when a threat approaches.

On the following pages, I want to share with you 20 important principles I have learned and applied in my career that can guide you into becoming the best of the best and a Top Gun in the corporate, institutional or government world.

During 35 years in the active military, reserves and the federal government, I encountered a small handful of truly incompetent managers. I also had the privilege of observing a couple of visionary leaders. Mostly, I saw average managers and leaders who were satisfied to plod along and pin their hopes on their charm and ability to cling to the coattails of real leaders.

You can learn from bad bosses as well as good ones. When I saw a manager or commander whose department was floundering and whose personnel were under achieving, I almost always saw disturbing warning signs such as a lack of pride and low morale. I never believed it was the fault of that commander. Instead, it was the fault of the person who placed him or her in that command position. If you have to hire your wife's cousin, Bubba, don't put him in a position where he can make the lives of your valuable personnel miserable. Your personnel are too important. If they believe you have their best interest at heart, they will work their fingers to the bone to excel. If you ever mislead them, they will never trust you again.

People can take away your money and your life; they can take your dignity and dreams; but they can never take your integrity. *That* you must consciously and freely give. No promotion, nothing in life is worth your integrity. Guard it.

I considered naming this book "Top Gun *Leadership"* but I believe "Management" is a more accurate term. It characterizes the personnel and/or process of leading and directing all or part of an organization through the deployment and manipulation of resources. Those resources can be human, financial, material, intellectual or intangible. The word "manage" comes from the Italian *maneggiare* which means "to handle" — especially a horse, which in turn derives from the Latin *manus* which means "hand." Management refers to power by position, whereas leadership involves power by influence.

As you struggle in your battle for supremacy, it is my hope that this book will provide you with some tools and weaponry to include in your arsenal. Keep your powder dry and may God bless you.

Captain McVay in front of an F-100 Super Saber in 1975

Chapter One:

There is No One Like You

I grew up barefoot among the lakes and clear rivers of North Central Arkansas during the happy days of the mid twentieth century. I was 11 when Chevrolet unveiled their first Corvette, the 1953 six-cylinder. Two years later the Ford Thunderbird appeared. My family was poor but an idyllic environment combined with great neighbors and friends made for a very happy childhood in the great town of Mountain Home. My childhood dream was to one day own a Corvette.

I loved school – not because of academics but for many other reasons. I was involved in several extracurricular activities which included playing starting center for the Mountain Home Varsity basketball team, the *Bombers*. I had even received scholarship offers from a couple of small in-state colleges. Shortly after graduation and upon return from our senior trip to Washington, DC and New York City, my world was turned upside down. I was riding with a classmate in a borrowed MGA roadster when she lost control on a curve and plunged down a 30 foot embankment. The car hit passenger-side down, throwing the driver downward onto me and into the metal behind my seat. She was killed instantly. My right shoulder was dislocated and it felt like my back was broken. I put my shoulder back in place (a decision I later regretted), stood up, and climbed the embankment. The accident that cost my dear friend her life, cost me my free ticket to college, and greatly restricted the movement of my right arm.

Despite my injury, I was allowed to keep my lifeguard position at the municipal swimming pool but worked mainly in the concession stand. I once made the mistake of relieving the lifeguard on duty so he could receive a phone call. My shoulder had not healed and I was clearly not fit for lifeguard duty. But as luck would have it, this would be the only time during my two summers as a lifeguard that I would have to rescue a swimmer. A little boy had talked another boy into swimming across the deep end of the pool. When out in the middle, one panicked and grabbed the other around the neck. Both were struggling under water when I jumped in to pull them both out of the pool. That singular incident added weeks to my healing time and turned my arm and shoulder black and blue.

After that summer I took a temporary job with the Army and Air Force Exchange Service (AAFES) in Omaha where my brother lived. I simultaneously applied for a job with Western Electric. A week after applying, I stopped by the front office to check on the status of my application. The personnel clerk couldn't find it and asked when I had applied. She then proceeded to dig through a stack of unfilled applications 2 feet high in order to locate mine. I was hired on the spot and put to work forming cables for switchboards. I soon quit the job and returned to Mountain Home. After a couple weeks passed, my friend, Phil Bradley and I decided we would go to Kansas City and apply for a job with General Motors. We applied on a Monday and went to work on Tuesday. The pay was nice and the people were friendly but I couldn't see outside. I was bothered because I didn't know if it was day or night, raining or sunny. After a couple of months, Phil and I decided to join the Air Force.

I aimed high and set my sights on becoming an officer and pilot. That was such an improbable goal that after spending several years pursuing it, my buddy looked me in the eyes one day and said, "Mack, you are just reaching for the stars." My response was, "Maybe so Bradley, but somebody has got to fly those jets and it might as well be me." During my four-year Air Force enlistment I became an Intelligence Analyst. The technical school lasted nine months at Goodfellow, AFB in San Angelo, Texas and was followed by my first operational assignment on the extreme northern tip of Hokkaido Island at Wakkanai, Japan.

I had three nominations to attend the United States Air Force Academy, one each from Congressman James W. Trimble, Senator J. William Fulbright and a nomination from the Air Force itself. During the extensive examination process at Tokyo, my shoulder injury prevented me from attending the academy. It did, however, get me an operation that restored movement to my right shoulder and three weeks in the Tachikawa AFB Hospital for physical therapy. The following year I was too old to enter the academy.

During my 13 month tour at Wakkanai I studied Japanese Language by attending the University of Maryland Far East Division. Later, after having received credits from the University of Maryland Far East Division, I was able to attend that university's home campus while stationed at the National Security Agency in Maryland.

I quickly fell in love with the Japanese People. We had terrific maid service in the dormitories and I developed a matronly relationship with some of the maids. One dear old Japanese lady who spoke almost no English cried the day I left.

I took advantage of every educational opportunity in the Air Force and after four years of service, I was only one semester shy of an Associate's Degree. I left the Air Force and attended Southern Baptist Junior College in Walnut Ridge, Arkansas for that semester. The college is now a four year institution named Williams College. I believe in education and I also believe that education should never end.

While attending Southern Baptist College, I began my flying career by training in an old Piper Super Cruiser tail dragger. Shortly after earning an Associate of Arts degree, I obtained a Private Pilot's License and applied for USAF pilot training with the Air National Guard. My timing was finally right and I was accepted to replace an officer who failed the entrance physical. It wasn't until I was actually attending undergraduate pilot training at Vance Air Force Base in Enid, Oklahoma that I learned that out of 1,000 applicants only one actually graduates to wear the silver wings of an Air Force Pilot. Before we got our hands on an Air Force jet, we flew civilian light aircraft to test our flying skills and our ability to follow instructions. That initial phase of training saw the loss of 40% of my class. This occurred during a period when the Air Force had a huge pilot shortage. Most of my classmates were engineers, but some were lawyers. Two students at Vance had PhDs and were training to become astronauts.

It was common knowledge among the trainees that "Everybody flunks a check ride" and we were told not to worry when that happens. "You always get a recheck and then an elimination ride before they wash you out of the program." I guess I was the only class member who did not flunk a single check ride. I loved every minute of pilot training. I had been paying to take flying lessons in a $5,000 airplane and now the Air Force was paying *me* to fly million dollar supersonic jets. Shortly before graduation, because of a severe pilot shortage during the Vietnam War, I was offered my choice of assignments if I would volunteer for two years of Air Force active duty. I agreed without hesitation and selected the new C-141 Starlifter. The 141 was the most sophisticated transport of the time and the first choice of my classmates who finished at the top of the class. I would have picked a fighter, but the training would have required most of the two years and I knew the opportunity to fly fighters would still exist once I returned to the Air National Guard. I was surprised to learn that my Guard Commander was unaware of the Air Force offer and questioned "by what authority" I was ordered to active duty. My orders read "Headquarters United States Air Force by direction of The President."

During the two year active duty tour I flew the maximum time allowed by regulations, 110 hours per month. Most of my flights were in and out of Vietnam. I saw much of South Vietnam including Saigon, Da Nang Pleiku, Phu Cat, Bien Hoa, and Cam Ranh Bay. I recall my first trip to Cam Ranh Bay when the base came under rocket and sapper attack. In Vietnam the sappers were special operations soldiers who used infiltration, sabotage, and ambush to attack our forces. I was standing on the ramp next to my airplane when the fireworks began. I asked the surly old maintenance sergeant servicing my jet if he thought we should get into one of the bunkers that rimmed the parking apron. "There are rats in those bunkers," he replied.

As a First Lieutenant I was selected to upgrade to Global Qualified Aircraft Commander. I think I was the only First Lieutenant ever qualified to fly Air Evacuation flights. Air Evac flights are the highest priority flights in the Air Force and take precedence over Air Force One. They involve turning the aircraft into a hospital with doctors and nurses to care for up to a hundred patients. A few First Lieutenants were upgraded to Aircraft Commander but not early enough to become Air Evac qualified before making Captain.

Newly upgraded aircraft commanders were required to fly with an aircraft commander qualified copilot for the first 100 hours. In my case this requirement was waived and my first overseas flight was with a brand new second pilot.

My wing commander, Brigadier General James Hill called me into his office and congratulated me on my upgrade. He told me that I would be in command of officers vastly senior to myself and that I should know that he would stand behind my decisions. He further told me that if I had a crew member who did not perform up to my standards, I could send him home from anywhere in the world and he would send me a replacement.

I had great respect for General Hill. Ten years later I was on the board of the National Guard Association of Arkansas on my way to becoming president. I invited General Hill to be keynote speaker at our annual conference. By that time he was a four star general and vice chief of staff of the Air Force. He accepted the invitation but two months before the conference he was forced to cancel because President Jimmy Carter had nominated him for retirement. He retired in 1980 with 37 years service.

We worked long days and nights in those days, sometimes 24 hours straight. While airline pilots had to be checked out on each specific route, I recall flying as the aircraft commander into countries where no member of the crew had ever set foot before. There were regular missions to Europe and the Caribbean as well as the Far East. My last scheduled mission was to take the Embassy flight around the world through Australia, New Deli, and Spain. Unfortunately, however, my squadron lost that mission to a new Reserve Associate Squadron at Travis, AFB. I enjoyed the challenge and excitement of global flying and could have been happy with a career in the Air Force. During those two years I was credited with fifty combat missions in Southeast Asia and awarded 7 medals and decorations.

I was encouraged to remain on active and recommended for a regular commission. I elected to return to the Arkansas Air National Guard in Fort Smith, Arkansas. The 188th Tactical Reconnaissance Group was flying RF-84s. Soon after I arrived home, the unit learned the 84s would be replaced with the RF-101 Voodoo. The F-101 had set the world speed record of 1,207 mph on December 12, 1957. Air force pilots were not allowed to fly the 101 until they had 750 hours experience in other aircraft. I convinced the commander to send me to RF-101 training rather than have me check out in the 84. He allowed me to attend the nine-month long training course which included the combat training necessary to become fully qualified and combat ready. I therefore became the first pilot in the Group to be certified "combat ready" in the jet. While still a First Lieutenant, I became an instructor. To my knowledge, I was the only First Lieutenant IP in the history of the F-101.

Air National Guard units are comprised of mostly part-time personnel with full time civilian jobs like airline pilots, high school superintendents, insurance salesmen and people from all walks of life including medical doctors and ministers. Some of the members are full-time federal employees called "technicians." I was offered an airline job but declined in order to become a full time employ of the Air National Guard. By this time, I was serving as a Captain and had completed my military education well in advance of my grade. This education included Squadron Officer School and Air Command and Staff College. As a full time federal employee in the grade of GS-13 who had completed Command and Staff College, I was qualified to enroll in the Air War College by correspondence. As a Captain, I became the first member of the 188th to complete the War College and possibly the first company grade officer to complete any war college. After 35 years of service, I retired as a Colonel and Command Pilot.

The most responsibility ever given to me was command of a multinational Provisional Wing equipped with $3 billion worth of Army, Navy, Air Force, Marine Corps and Canadian Air Force fighters, bombers, tankers, cargo and AWACS aircraft. In fact, I was the first Air National Guard officer selected to command such a wing. The assignment was widely reported in publications such as *The Air Force Times* and *Air Force Magazine.*

During Vietnam, the tankers had a commander; the bombers had another commander, and so on. Under this system, one commander often had to request, indeed, beseech another commander for support. I was among the handful of Colonels and Generals charged with the task of restructuring the Air National Guard into a single-commander-led, multi-component organizational model. When I had the privilege of commanding the new type of wing, I fully appreciated the utility and performance of the creation.

Developing the modern structure was not easy.

We had to avoid turf battles and shift deeply ingrained paradigms. During Desert Storm, we witnessed the effectiveness of three Provisional Wings as they drove the Iraqi Army out of Kuwait.

Just before retirement I was offered a General Officer position on the Arkansas Air National Guard State Staff. Mike Huckabee had recently become governor following the conviction of Governor Jim Guy Tucker for fraud during the Whitewater scandal. The position I was offered had very little authority and did not interest me. I was becoming dissolutioned with the governor. Within hours of his ascendancy to the office of governor, Mike Huckabee's wife Janet was in Nova Scotia visiting my Engineering Squadron at their deployed location. I was surprised that the first lady would be on a junket so soon. I have long noted that politicians and their wives will travel eagerly to Las Vegas, the Gulf Coast or outside the country to visit military units. These same politicians often will not walk across the street to visit the same units.

Early in 1997 I began to contemplate a run for governor. I am a fifth generation Arkansan and would love to help my beloved state. I wanted to restructure Arkansas government to make it efficient. The state has 53 Cabinet level departments and a convoluted organizational chart that looks like a maze from *Alice in*

Wonderland. At the time, the state was 49th in per capita income but an amazing 12th in taxes paid per dollar earned. I was most disturbed that the low-income citizens of Arkansas had to pay a 10% sales tax on groceries. It saddens me to see an elderly person on a fixed income reach into a change purse to pay for a loaf of bread, a bottle of milk *and* an additional 10% for an inefficient state government. Sometimes a mother had to return an item because she did not have enough money left after the tax was added. Arkansas also had 310 school districts with the same number of superintendents; one county with a total population of 5,000 had four superintendents.

I shared my vision for streamlining Arkansas government with some members of the Legislature. By that time many began to see the governor as a liberal in Republican clothing. Nevertheless, the Republicans were giddy over having a Republican in office and didn't look very far beyond that achievement. Since the governor was unelected and had been thrust into office under difficult circumstances, most citizens believed he deserved a chance as an elected governor.

I was reaching the conclusion that Abraham Lincoln would not be able to beat Mike Huckabee in 1998. When I first shared my assessment with John Cross, one of my best friends, he practically got on his knees and begged me not to make a decision yet. He told me that he would fly me around the state in his airplane during the campaign. Some members of the Arkansas Legislature also continued to urge me to run. I agreed to keep an open mind.

John and his wife joined me for Church services at the First Baptist Church of Fort Smith one Sunday. Two days later, on August 12th, 1997, my close friend and his wife Joy were killed in a plane crash at Alice, Texas. He had been an Air National Guard Squadron Commander and fighter pilot as well as an airline captain with thousands of hours in the air. Joy was also a commercial pilot and a third commercial pilot from Fort Smith was also onboard. Another pilot was flying the twin engine turboprop when both propellers had a dramatic RPM loss immediately after lift off from the runway. I was shopping at Sam's Club when I received a phone call from my friend's boss telling me about the crash.

The tragedy dominated my life for many weeks while I helped the children make arrangements and pull their lives together. The family requested a funeral fly by and that request was denied. Not only was my friend a former military command pilot, he was also a member of the airport commission. I would not take "no" for an answer. With involvement from my congressman, the missing man fly by request was finally approved.

After the funeral a crisis developed when Joy's son decided not to return to Baylor University for a semester. I told him that not returning to school would not be a wise decision. I phoned Baylor and explained the situation. I was told to tell him to contact a specific person there and not to worry about finances. Baylor stood ready to do what was necessary including the procurement Pell Grants. Once back at Baylor I was in frequent contact until I was able to move the life insurance process to a successful conclusion.

John's sons are adults. One is an airline pilot and the other is a petroleum engineer.. John was so proud of them. They were determined to find out what had caused the crash and did not waiver until they were able to learn all the details and obtain a settlement for the families involved.

When I turned my attention back to the gubernatorial decision, I was disposed to honor John's wishes and enter the race. As word spread that I might become a candidate, the Arkansas Republican Party doubled the filing fee to $10,000 -- I suppose to discourage competition.

When the smoke cleared, my opponent had spent

over a million dollars on the primary race. That was 33 times more money than I spent. He crushed me in the primary and his democratic challenger in the general election. All in all, it was a wonderful experience that gave me the opportunity to meet a lot of very nice people.

To say I was disappointed in the 10 years Mike Huckabee was in office would be an understatement. Mike Huckabee has been criticized for his fiscal record as governor having increased state spending 65.3% from 1996 to 2004 and supporting numerous tax hikes. The CATO Institute gave him an F grade for spending and tax policy in 2006, and an overall grade of D for his governorship. Only one other republican received an F while five received As and Bs. Mike Huckabee granted clemency 669 times which is more than the 507 clemencies given by the three previous governors combined. Many of the clemencies were granted to convicted murderers.

I have never regretted running for statewide office and meeting so many nice people.. I like nice people who can be comfortable being themselves. That brings us to

Top Gun Management Principle Number One: Be Yourself.

Too many upwardly mobile executives feel they need to be somebody else or act like somebody else. George Patton and Omar Bradley were distinguished generals but outright opposites. Bradley was known as the "solder's general" while Patton was known as "Old Blood and Guts." Sometimes you have to do what works. Don't use a push when a nudge will work. Dress for success but do you really need to go deeply into debt to buy that luxury SUV?

Take, for example, three billionaires. When Sam Walton was the richest man in America, he drove an old Ford pickup truck. Billionaire and presidential candidate Ross Perot drove a ten-year-old Oldsmobile. I remember inviting my friend, Lieutenant Governor Win Rockefeller, to speak in Fort Smith. At the time, his net worth was $1.3 billion. After speaking to my civic club, I drove him to the radio station for an interview and then to an elementary school where Win was scheduled to talk to some third grade students and read them a book. Afterward, the first question came from a little boy who asked Win if he had a limousine. Governor Rockefeller told the boy he did not own a limousine. The little boy persisted, "Did you come over here in a limousine?" he asked. Governor Rockefeller said he had not come in a limousine; he had ridden in Mr. McVay's Chevrolet van.

The little boy then wanted to know what kind of car Win Rockefeller owned. Win told him he owned a Chevrolet pickup.

While writing this book I was listening to the Radio Factor with Bill O'Reilly in the background. O'Reilly is one of the most successful contemporary authors as well as radio and television broadcast journalists of all time. He was talking about driving a five-year-old vehicle. I could imagine a middle manager pulling up next to him at a stop light in an expensive SUV and feeling a little bit sorry for the poor guy in the five year old car.

This is a long story to tell you to save your money. Don't buy a vehicle you can't afford. Don't find yourself one paycheck away from the poor house. Don't impress billionaires with your fancy car. Live within your means. The people driving cars they can't afford in order to impress other people who are driving cars they can't afford only end up impressing each other.

This quote by the great educator George Washington Carver dates to the first half of the last century, "We have become 99% money mad. The method of living at home modestly and within our income, laying a little by systematically for the proverbial rainy day which is due to come, can almost be listed among the lost arts." If you identify with this statement, you are likely among the majority of Americans who are deeply in debt. Things have not improved since Professor Carver uttered those words.

Getting out from under the weight of indebtedness requires many of the attributes possessed by top gun managers, not the least of which is courage. Debt problems must be attacked aggressively and decisively. You can and must achieve debt supremacy. The very best time to start is at this very moment. Make this a top priority.

Work cheerfully together with your coworkers and enjoy their camaraderie. Don't try to act like a big shot. Don't spend all your time trying to get into the good graces of important people; enjoy the company of ordinary people. Do things in such a manner so that everyone can see you are being honest not only with them, but with yourself as well. Respect the young, aged, weak and strong. During your lifetime, you will have been all of these.

Every single member of my staff had a much larger and more expensive house than I had. I was fortunate enough to retire at age 54 with no debt.

Chapter Two:

Who's the Fairest of Them All?

If you insist on getting credit for all the great ideas, over time you will have to produce all the great ideas yourself. On the other hand, if you don't care who gets the credit and are willing to give credit where credit is due, you will succeed. This brings us to

Top Gun Management Principle Number Two: Surround Yourself with People Smarter than You.

I admit that I have been tempted to hire people I like over applicants who are more qualified. It is difficult to tell a friend that you will be hiring someone else. Nevertheless, that is what I did: hired the most qualified. While I didn't realize all the ramifications at the time, I was doing both people a favor.

When I look at potential employees, I look at the whole person. Too many companies only recruit from the top universities in the world. There are certainly places for those with MBAs from Ivy League Universities. Yet, Wal-Mart and Microsoft were built by Sam Walton and Bill Gates.

Sam grew up during the depression and worked his way through the University of Missouri. It was his drive that lifted Wal-Mart above the Gibson's Discount Centers and Magic Marts into the stratosphere. Bill Gates did attend Harvard but left during his third year to craft his $285 billion dollar company.

The service academies have produced some great leaders; however, one of the contemporary veterans I most admire did not graduate from West Point. He was born in the New York City neighborhood of Harlem and was raised in the South Bronx. He graduated from public school in The Bronx and received a bachelor's degree from City College of New York attaining a 'C' average. He later obtained an MBA from The George Washington University after his second tour in Vietnam. That person is former Chairman of the Joint Chiefs of Staff and Secretary of State Colin Powell. My personal belief is that the Iraq War would have been handled better if Colin Powell's expertise had been utilized more.

I am quite sure that you are familiar with situations where everyone likes all their coworkers and the entire group functions together like a well-oiled machine. They get pretty good at setting type and using the linotype machine while members of the firm across the street have junked their linotypes and started employing new photo typesetters.

But, just because you hire all the bright people you can afford does not mean you are out of the woods yet.

Top Gun Principle Number Three: Communicate.

I don't mean to be trite. All top executives think they are great communicators. I have told my staff more than once, "If I am doing something wrong or going down the wrong path, tell me. I may not always agree but I promise to always listen."

I remained true to my word and listened. Everybody from the bottom to the top knew they could walk into my office and tell me I was wrong and I would listen. If I persisted in being stupid they would persist in telling me. I would always continue to listen. This is certainly an alien concept to a multitude of executives, especially those whose motto is "My way or the highway." Those decisive leaders who make Custer-type decisions and stick with them to the loss of all else will never understand the value of listening. You can't listen with your mouth open. Your associates, employees, suppliers, and customers all have something valuable to say. You will never learn what it is if you drown them out by talking all the time. Remember, if you do all the talking, you can only learn what you already know. Shut up and learn.

When I made a decision, my staff always worked hard to make it work. Open and frank communications does not lead to anarchy or a lack of leadership. Instead, it lets you know when you are truly doing the right thing and nothing is being overlooked. Tests have shown that several people can guess the number of beans in a jar and while no one person may guess the correct number, the average of all the guesses will likely be correct. While experts were trying to figure out how to dislodge a trailer truck from beneath an overpass, a young boy suggested letting the air out of the tires. A staff member may be wrong a hundred times before hitting a home run, but he or she will never hit the ball unless given the opportunity to try. With freedom of expression, a good idea from one person can turn into a great idea with input from the group.

If you want to stop communication, all you have to do is tell someone that the decision has been made and is final. If you want to limit debate, tell someone that his or her idea is stupid or pointless. That person will keep silent in the future, even if your hair catches on fire.

Can you take criticism? Does listening to a lowly employee take away from your authority? Do you already have all the answers? The people who will get you fired are not your superiors but your subordinates. Listen to them.

If you manage people, work in Human Resources, or care about your friends and colleagues, chances are good that one day you will need to face a difficult communication situation. Not all people are perfect, so some may dress inappropriately for work. Personal grooming can sometimes be improper. Flirtatious and suggestive behavior can lead to sexual harassment troubles. Earthy language is unprofessional and unbecoming. Revealing dress may be acceptable at a club, a party or on the beach, but has no place in a professional work environment.

These are just examples of the types of behavior that demand responsible and considerate feedback with tact and discretion. Even though you are the boss you should be very diplomatic. You might start by telling the employee that you have some feedback you'd like to share. Ask "Is now a good time to talk, or would you prefer to select another time and place?"

Use a non-threatening gentle entry. Give the person a chance to brace for potentially embarrassing criticism. Tell the employee that you need to provide feedback that is difficult and uncomfortable to share. Most managers are as uncomfortable correcting an individual for poor personal dress or habits as the person receiving the correction.

Often, you are placed in this role because other employees have complained to you about the individual's habit, behavior, or dress. There is no need to mention this and therefore heighten the embarrassment. The objective is to correct the bad tendency and facilitate a fast recovery for the person receiving feedback.

The last element that should be accomplished before concluding a difficult communication session is to reach an agreement about how and when the individual will change their behavior.

Communication is reciprocal. Remember that people are not mushrooms. Mushrooms flourish very well when kept in the dark and fed fertilizer. Employees, on the other hand, don't function very well when isolated. To be effective, your staff must know what you know. Everyone wants to feel like a member of the "in-crowd." When they have access to information as quickly as the rest of the group, they will respond like trusted colleagues.

Chapter Three:

What's the Problem?

As a leader, you can't fix a problem unless you know what it is. You may have a division chief who claims to have a problem. The problem is that he or she is working hard. To fix the problem, the chief needs someone else to do the work. If you had someone else to do the work you wouldn't need the division chief. That problem is not a problem. We elect our government leaders to serve us but too often they end up serving the bureaucrats. How does that happen you ask? Bureaucrats are experts at telling congressmen and cabinet members what they want them to know. Too few leaders know what questions they need to ask. That is why the government rarely performs as efficiently as private enterprise. The bureaucrat wants more money and more personnel when more efficiency and a much, much better work ethic would suffice.

Top Gun Management Principle Number Four: Understand the Problem.

Dr. Martin Luther King, Jr. said, "Shallow understanding from people of good will is more frustrating than absolute misunderstanding from people of ill-will."

The ordinary manager may see a lack of capital, low worker morale or poor quality as problems in the company. In fact, these are symptoms of the real problem: poor leadership and management. These are not the only signs that point directly to weak and ineffectual management. Countless businesses have failed because of a failure to recognize the real problem.

You will never solve problems unless you truly understand their depth and scope. This may not be readily apparent. The aircraft accident investigation process offers excellent insight into problem solving. Consider for instance that a bolt failed causing the aircraft to crash.

This is the obvious immediate cause, but what caused the bolt to fail? Was the bolt damaged, did it fail to meet manufacturing specifications or did the pilot overstress the aircraft during maneuvering?

A top gun manager anticipates problems in advance. One approach to understanding potential problems is to individually ask the members of your staff what performance elements are required to help them excel at their job. A real leader is not too preoccupied gazing at the horizon to look down and boost the production of an employee or associate. Am I suggesting that you roll up your sleeves and get your hands dirty? Yes. If the answer you receive involves throwing money at an issue, you might have a bigger problem. Likely, no one has ever asked that question of your employee before and the answer may be inaccurate.

Don't be afraid to request an audit. Many managers fear auditors; I used them to assist in achieving excellence. If you are afraid to request an audit of your operation, *you* have a problem.

Once you truly understand the problem, fix it. Don't waste time pointing fingers.

Often you will find that you have found the problem and the problem is you. You may be letting the bean counters take over operations. Your staff may be buried in unnecessary red tape. Your own rule to correct a minor problem may create a major problem. Get out of the office and find out what is going on. Don't depend on others to tell you, they may slant the truth. On the other hand, if everything runs as smoothly as a Japanese watch while you eat up all the travel funds attending charm schools, perhaps the company doesn't need you.

If a major problem develops in your sphere of responsibility it is your fault! If you knew about the problem and did nothing, it is your fault. If you did not know about the problem, it is your fault. Ignorance is not an excuse.

Top Gun Management Principle Number Five: Accept Responsibility.

There are many that are willing to accept the pay, the power, the prestige and the perks associated with top leadership positions. They love the travel and adventure. They cherish the two secretaries and the administrative assistant. They delight in the private bathroom, the big desk, the nice view from the corner office and the expense account. There is just something about power. Humans prefer power over anything else. That is why so many are eager to take huge pay cuts to become Cabinet Secretaries. Accepting the power and the perks comes easy, accepting the responsibility is another matter.

Josiah Charles Stamp was President of the Bank of England and the second richest man in Great Britain in the 1920s. He said, "It is easy to dodge our responsibilities, but we cannot dodge the consequences of dodging our responsibilities."

Too many top executives insulate themselves from responsibility. They always have someone to blame and that someone is certainly not themselves. They will influence a subordinate to take some action, then fire or at the very lease demote him or her when the project fails miserably. Equally as heinous is the exec who doesn't know what is going on around him but becomes appalled, incensed and indignant when he is in some way made aware. The blame goes to some poor supervisor who was doing the best he could with the guidance available.

It is time for you to face these facts previously stressed, if you knew what was going on, you are guilty, if you did not know what was going on, you are guilty.

You are responsible and must start accepting the responsibility. There is only one who lived on this earth who was perfect and you are not He. If you are working hard in the pursuit of excellence you will make mistakes.

The key is to learn from those mistakes and move on. Surgeons adopted the philosophy of ultimate personal responsibility many years ago. The evaluation of poor surgical outcomes during a traditional Morbidity and Mortality conference is based on a surgeon's sense of personal responsibility for what takes place in the operating theater. Regardless of equipment malfunctions, a scrub nurse who breaks sterile technique or an anesthetist who misdoses medication, the surgeon will always focus first on how he or she could have prevented the error and how they can be certain it will not happen again. When you go before the boss, the board or your electorate, admit your mistakes. It takes a mature person to do so. Take off the Teflon® coating and earn your paycheck.

William Penn, the founder of Pennsylvania said, "No man is fit to command another that cannot command himself." Until you shoulder the responsibility you will never have the respect necessary to run an excellent organization.

Chapter Four:

Reward, Reward, Reward

There are few things more discouraging than a thankless job. Old Joe has been with the company 40 years. He never misses a day of work and does a good job. Have you ever thought of thanking Joe for his faithfulness? A little attention and a pat on the back from the boss can be more meaningful than many leaders will ever understand.

Some executives have the attitude that people are expected to do their jobs or they get fired. That idea is going the way of the pay phone. And too often, the policy is "punish the innocent, promote the guilty and reward the uninvolved." In actual practice, rewarding an undeserving employee can do more harm to the work environment than you can imagine. Give praise where praise is due and you will foster a magnificent and productive work

Lieutenant Colonel McVay presenting the Eagle
Award to the outstanding officer in 1988

atmosphere that will likely lead to pronounced departmental or company-wide success.

If you have ever received a pat on the back for something you did, you know the feeling a little recognition can give you. There are people who work hard for 40 years and never receive any praise. Praise is cheap but you would think it costs a fortune.

Top Gun Management Principle Number Six: Recognize Excellence.

It has been proven that praise, more than money, is a motivator. Praise can take many forms and can go up as well as down. Some executives surround themselves with "yes" men so they can hear praise all the time. They can fall on their face and their staff will sing out in unison, "Well done!"

A great way to recognize excellence is to present an award. An award can be a certificate printed on card stock or a trophy. It can be a previously established award or one of your own creations. When I was president of the National Guard Association of Arkansas, I invented a prestigious award that I named the Archibald Yell Award. Yell was the first Congressman elected from Arkansas. He had served as a Territorial Judge after fighting alongside Andrew Jackson during the Battle of New Orleans. Yell was elected governor after a term in Congress and was then reelected to Congress.

When war broke out with Mexico, Yell walked out of Congress and enlisted in the Arkansas National Guard. Zachary Taylor is called the hero of Buena Vista, but Archibald Yell should be credited for the victory. Colonel Yell surrounded himself with some of his bravest men. Although vastly outnumbered, Yell stormed the middle of the Mexican line. When the dust cleared, the Mexicans were in full retreat. The inexperienced Arkansas Regiment had met Antonio Lopez de Santa Anna's veterans and won. Archibald Yell lay mortally wounded. Disparaging remarks from Albert Pike (who was defeated when Yell was elected Colonel) kept Yell from receiving the recognition he was due. You won't see a statue of Colonel Yell or a Congressman Yell Building in Washington, DC. Nevertheless, I was proud to name an award after a great Congressman who was killed in action while fighting for his country. The Archibald Yell Award is in the possession of a former President of The United States and a former Chief of the National Guard.

Can you imagine a United States Congressman or Senator walking out of the legislature and enlisting in the military during a time of war?

I can't count the number of awards I have presented including countless military decorations such as the Legion of Merit and The Outstanding Unit Citation. Keep a record of the awards you have already issued; the subsequent nominations become easier. Even as a retiree, you can still recognize excellence. As an officer in The American Legion, I have been honored to present scores of awards and certificates such as the Distinguished Americanism Award to Legionnaires who are still serving America as members of America's largest veterans' organization.

The award list also includes mayors, outstanding ROTC Cadets, outstanding students, and even a cabinet undersecretary. There is, however, one award that does not excite me, despite its explosive popularity in the world of management. I do not endorse nor encourage its use. It is the "Employee of the Month" award. Employees of the month have special parking spaces and have their pictures prominently posted. They may even have lunch with their boss and receive a nice certificate. In theory, this award would be moderately acceptable if it were based on measurable performance. In practice, however, it more often resembles a popularity contest. The true employee of the month probably deserves the award most every time, yet during the year there will be twelve different recipients.

You should be able to recognize excellence. Don't confuse excellence with glossy mediocrity. Too many managers confuse kissing up with job savvy. Don't be guilty of such. If you choose to reward someone for being a "yes" man, make that fact clear to other employees. If you recognize and promote excellence, then excellence will proliferate. If you recognize and promote "good old boys" who drink with you on your lunch break, you may drop out of the list of Fortune 500 Companies.

Instructor Pilot Lieutenant McVay and an RF-101
Voodoo in the early 1970s

Chapter Five:

It's Not About You

Top Gun Management Principle Number Seven: Value Your Human Capital.

When a machine breaks we know what to do: fix it. Humans are infinitely more complex than machines. They have good days and bad days. They are rarely at the top of their game 24/7. If one of your employees makes a mistake trying to fix a problem and this costs the company a lot of money, what do you do? Do you fire someone for trying to do their job? One such employee told his boss he should be fired after causing his company to lose five million dollars. His boss responded, "Fire you? I just spent five million dollars training you!" In the course of fixing problems, mistakes will be made. "To err is Human." People who don't make mistakes don't do anything. Don't encourage mistakes, but don't overreact to them either.

Today's professional environment is disturbingly bereft of loyalty. The headhunters are having a field day enticing executives to change jobs. This game of musical chairs does not seem to bother a lot of CEOs because they just steal another body from another corporation. They have a vacancy in accounting so they find a warm body and pat themselves on the back. After all, they barely knew the accounting executive anyway and will probably not waste any effort getting to know the new one. Sure, there will be an extensive interview process and references will be thoroughly checked and the new guy will have all the right answers, they always do. The best prospect may not be good at interviews, but the CEO has bigger fish to fry. After all, there is that upcoming conference on the French Riviera …

Take note of how the Israelis value their people. On June 27, 1976 the world watched with rapt attention when four terrorists made the mistake of hijacking Air France Flight 139. It originated in Tel Aviv, Israel and was carrying 248 passengers and a crew of 12. There was no doubt that Israel would not stand and watch their citizens held hostage at Entebbe Airport.

I doubt that the world actually knows the real story of the rescue. It was indeed my privilege to hear the story from the officer who was given the responsibility of rescuing the hostages and flying the lead C-130. His squadron rented a white Mercedes and rigged it to look like Uganda President Idi Amin's automobile (this required painting it black, to the chagrin of the owner). The Israelis landed the C-130s shortly before midnight without lights and offloaded the Mercedes along with Range Rovers. Pulling up in front of the terminal, the Israelis swooped from their vehicles and erupted into the terminal yelling, "Get down! Get down!" in Hebrew and English. The hostages were quickly loaded onto a C-130, but then the flight leader received a radio call that there was not enough room on the airplane for their squadron vehicle. It was an old Peugeot valued at only a few hundred dollars. The Lieutenant Colonel's response was simple and direct. He ordered them to make room for that Peugeot, "that is our Peugeot!" In the end, the old Peugeot did not become the property of Idi Amin.

The return flight was tense until the C-130s were met over the Red Sea by a flight of F-4 Phantoms armed to the hilt. It is always comforting to have a fighter escort.

I should mention in passing that the Israeli Government turned their operation over to the military. When the US had our own hostage situation in Iran about three years later, the rescue was planned in the White House. Despite the bureaucratic strategizing in the Oval Office, President Jimmy Carter told members of the military that they would be great heroes if the mission was successful. If the mission failed it would be a major embarrassment to The President. I learned this from a three star general who was present in the Oval Office. This ill-fated rescue attempt failed during a sand storm in the Great Salt Desert in Eastern Iran dooming the hostages to 444 days of fear and captivity.

There was a great difference in the handling of these two hostage situations. The Israelis told a military squadron what to do and let them do their job. The United States had involvement by The President himself.

Things work better when you tell people what you want, not how to get it done. You will find people more responsive and less defensive if you can give them guidance rather than instructions. You will also see more initiative, more innovation, and more of an attitude of ownership of projects.

The top gun manager values people the way the Israelis cherish theirs. That country is willing to go to war for the sake of one soldier. When your solders know you have their best interests in mind and are willing to go to the mat on their behalf, they will respond with loyalty and productivity. Your organization will become stronger and the headhunters will go home headless. The greatest leader of all time put it this way: "Do unto others as you would have others do unto you."

Top Gun Management Principle Number Eight: Coach and Mentor.

I strongly believe in the concept of *noblesse oblige*: "nobility obligates." This is stated in The Holy Scriptures in another way; Jesus said, "For unto whomsoever much is given, of him shall be much required" (Luke 12:48, KJV). The concept is generally used to imply that with wealth, power, and prestige come social responsibilities. While the term can be used with a derisive sense of condescending or hypocritical social responsibility, I prefer the more broadly applied use referring to those capable of simple acts doing so for the benefit of others.

On Christmas Day, 1962, I was spending my first Christmas outside the United States at Wakkanai, Japan. I entered the dining hall and began to eat Christmas dinner all alone. The dining hall was completely empty except for the cooks and staff. I was feeling a little sorry for myself when a civilian walked in and asked if he could join me. It was Raymond William Stacey Burr. At that time he was about half way through his hit TV series, *Perry Mason*, which won him two Emmy awards. What started as my worst Christmas dinner quickly became my most memorable.   The great actor was familiar with my hometown. He had fished many times in the Arkansas Ozarks.

Raymond Burr could have spent Christmas anywhere he pleased. He unselfishly chose to spend it on the northern tip of Japan with me.   He was a real Hollywood star who dated Natalie Wood and starred in movies, TV and radio. He was also a generous man. He donated his salary from the *Perry Mason* Movies to charity. He once sponsored 27 foster children through the Christian Children's Fund. He would take the children with the greatest medical needs. This is what I mean by *noblesse oblige.*

In 1995 I started a local program with Partners in Education called "Principal for a Day." That year I spent a day at an elementary school mentoring the children. I read to the first graders and showed third graders how airplanes fly. I had a long talk with a group of children with learning disabilities. When I left them they seemed highly motivated to succeed and excel. I think some will do well. The most rewarding part of my day was when I talked to the fifth graders. I warned them about the dangers of credit cards. I told them that if they begin saving at age twenty and save $170 a month invested at 10% interest, by the time they become 60 years old they will have a million dollars. I encouraged them to live within their means and not to spend more money than they earn. I told them that when I was their age my mother, father and brother all smoked cigarettes and they were all trying to quit. Many of my friends were smokers and all were trying to quit. I reasoned that if they were all trying to quit, perhaps I shouldn't start. That is a decision I have never regretted.

A few weeks later, a teacher delivered a stack of letters from the fifth graders. One letter was from a little girl:

Dear Colonel McVay,

When you came to our class, I thought you was a mean old man.

But you was cool.

Thanks for coming to our class.

I have never received a higher endorsement. I felt that I made a difference in a small way. The teacher told me that the kids kept asking how much money they would have by a certain date if they saved a certain amount. The teacher wore out her calculator.

An operations technician came to me one day and asked about a whole life insurance policy that a salesman was trying to sell her. I had a busy schedule that day: a briefing to be prepared for delivery that afternoon, two performance appraisals to write and several meetings with personnel. My "In" basket was full and my secretary was on vacation. In short, there was nothing more pressing than that young mother's questions. I pulled out a calculator and showed her the value of the whole life policy compared to the amount of money she could save by investing. Whole life is both a forced savings plan and life insurance and therefore pays less than other savings options. I advised her to open savings accounts for her two young daughters who would soon grow up and be thinking about college. After discussing specific amounts, she was surprised to see that with proper planning, college would be affordable. Before she left my office, we discussed buying homes and automobiles. I do not count the half-hour invested helping a valuable coworker as wasted time.

College and education are so important. How often have you heard that? I remember when my daughter announced that she was going to major in chemical engineering with aspirations for medical school. That way, she explained, if she failed to get acceptance to medical school, she would still be an engineer and easily able to support herself. It sounded logical to me. Today she is a Medical Doctor with a degree in Chemical Engineering on her way to becoming a Surgeon. She has also elected to serve her country for three years in the Air Force after residency training. I wish I could take credit for her success but the credit is all hers. Many parents do all they can for their children only to suffer heartbreak. I never fail to count my blessings.

I can't count the number of people I have counseled about retirement. I advised several to buy a savings bond every two weeks starting five years before retirement. That way a bond would mature every two weeks during the first five years of their retirement, helping with the transition. I am sad to say that too many people fail to plan for retirement. Others just can't make the decision to retire and work too long. I once explained to a colleague with 40 years of service that he was working for about a dollar an hour. The difference between his pay and his retirement pension was almost nothing. He has been retired for about ten years now and told me he was crazy for not retiring sooner.

I have never met a retiree who wished they would have worked longer. I retired when I was 54 years old and have enjoyed every second of my time. I considered buying an airplane; I had owned five different small airplanes during my younger days. My favorite was a Mooney Mark 21 which I flew into the Bermuda Triangle. The flight from Fort Lauderdale to Freeport on the Grand Bahama Island is actually only 90 miles – I noted no green fog or spinning instruments. The ground crew in Florida did tell me that several pilots get out of the sight of land and promptly return, thinking their engines are running rough.

After pondering the purchase of an airplane I decided I was in no hurry to go anywhere. I also reasoned that I had used up most of my luck during the preceding thirty years in the air. I bought a motor home instead that has given my family great pleasure. I discovered state and national parks and found that I actually enjoy fishing.

The "Principal for a Day" program has grown from one participant the first year to about a hundred now. I still participate along with the current crop of business and government leaders. My wife and I like to hike the great trails in Arkansas, Missouri and Oklahoma.

I'm an eBay Power Seller and Antique Dealer. I lecture before clubs and organizations about several diverse subjects such as the mysteries of Egypt and the Clayton Brothers (important but little-known figures in Arkansas' history). I am active in veterans' organizations locally and nationally. I support several worthy organizations and am past president of the local Crimestoppers organization and Heritage Foundation. Shortly after retirement I joined Mensa, the local historical society and some civic organizations.

After your family, try to carve out time for your church, your community and yourself.

An F-4 Phantom with the ancient Turkish city of
Pergamom in the background. Photo taken by Gene
McVay in the 1980s

Chapter Six:

PRIORITIZE

Wasting time has been elevated to a profession in America. Some managers confuse activity with production. "Busyness" does not equal productivity. I once had a manager who looked like he was running the whole world. His phone was always ringing. His desk was full of paperwork and he was given to bouts of ricocheting off the walls. He was an impressive person but never seemed to accomplish any meaningful work. Others spend the entire day working very hard on low priority tasks. As a Top Gun leader your time is extremely valuable. The future of your organization relies on your effectiveness and your effectiveness depends on your ability to make the best use of your time.

Top Gun Management Principle Number Nine: Optimize Your Time.

We have already discussed wasting your time performing public relations activities. There are things that you enjoy doing that really don't have to be done today. In fact, if you put those things off until next year nothing will be lost. As a general rule, spend some time getting organized and then focus on the top priorities and the big picture. You can't be effective running around putting out fires. Delegate the firefighting and second priority tasks to capable subordinates. Spend the bulk of your time prosecuting the big stuff. You may not enjoy the hard tasks but you and your organization will reap the rewards in the end. Don't spend five minutes on a tertiary task when you can spend that five minutes working on a top drawer problem. Time waits for no one. Countless books have been written about time management. As a self directed executive, only you can divine how best to use your time. Excellence in time management should be a top priority for every colleague within the realm of your influence. President Abraham Lincoln said, "You cannot escape the responsibility of tomorrow by evading it today." Some people reach the end of life only to realize that they wasted their whole lifetime. Make the best use of your time because you can never recycle wasted time.

Top Gun Management Principle Number Ten: Get Organized.

Planning and executing a bombing attack deep into enemy territory requires great organization and teamwork. This overwhelming task might look easy to a bystander because of the professionalism of the participants. The inciting event occurs when the command authority decides how to apportion their assets. Early in a conflict, most of the fighter assets might be committed to achieving air supremacy, say 80%. Fifteen percent might be used for support of ground troops while the remaining fighters might be employed for interdiction missions deep into enemy territory. Once air superiority is achieved, the percentages change. At a lower level of command, actual targets are selected using intelligence and imagery. The missions are communicated to Expeditionary Wings and their Squadrons in the form of an air tasking order. At the execution level, a mission planning cell converts the order into flight schedules complete with ordinance loads. By the time the fighter pilots are ready to brief, air refueling tankers may already be in the air and bombs already loaded on the aircraft. The targets and flight schedules as well as all known or suspected threats will also be in the hands of controllers aboard Airborne Warning and Control System or AWACS aircraft. The AWACS is a radar-based electronic system designed to carry out airborne surveillance, battle management, and command and control functions using modified Boeing 707 and 767 aircraft. All of these assets work for one commander. As one who functioned in that capacity, I fully appreciate the synergism gained when an AWACS controller can function as a distressed fighter's wingman rather than diverting other fighters from their missions. Without proper planning and organization, there would be little chance for success in the ensuring chaos.

One of my friends and colleagues never learned to type. In my world, not being able to type would be a momentous handicap. Even if you have two secretaries and an administrative assistant, typing is an essential skill. I am grateful that I took the time to develop a typing skill and to learn how to operate computers years ago.

Before Microsoft® introduced Windows®, I owned a Commodore 64 computer equipped with Microsoft

BASIC. By the time most of my friends finally purchased a computer, I had owned about a dozen. The biggest bargain on the planet is a personal computer. Today's $2,000 personal computer would have cost millions of dollars just a few decades ago. Purchasing one early in your career is a wise investment.

While education and training are important preparations, getting organized generally involves creating a system for common tasks and decisions. An essential ingredient in this process is a comprehensive and detailed planning process for normal and contingency operations. Leaders who refuse to take the time to prepare are disorganized by definition. With few or no systems or plans, they must make every decision on a case by case basis. Eventually this becomes tedious and frustrating. Professionals make the difficult seem routine and they do so by being organized.

President Abraham Lincoln said, "If I had eight hours to chop down a tree, I'd spend six hours sharpening my axe."

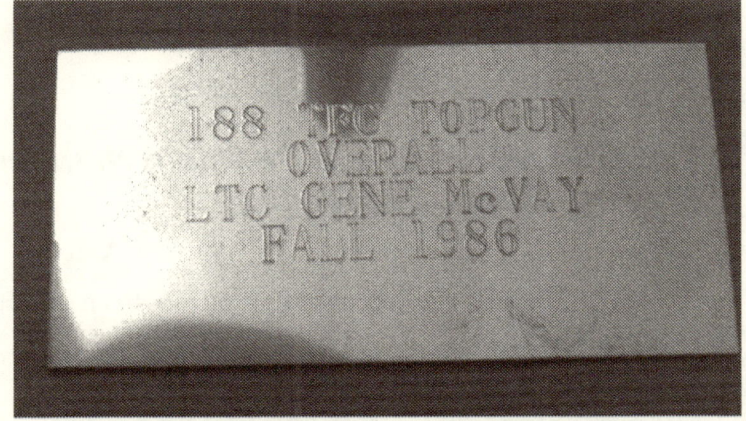

Chapter Seven:

We're #1

Top Gun Management Principle Number Eleven: Adopt Excellence.

Sure, one organization differs from another as one state is different than other states. Nevertheless, all states have things in common. Ever single state collects taxes but not all states have income tax. Some states have no sales tax. Alaska has different problems than Florida. All states issue driver's licenses and all have health departments. Some state has the best health department and the most streamlined driver's license procedures. If a state develops problems in the Department of Finance there are several ways to attack the issue. It can reinvent the wheel, or look for the state that has the most excellent Finance Department and adopt the features that will address the problem. This won't happen at the national conference of finance departments. This will happen through state to state cooperation. Improvement will come when improvement is sought. People fear change, but when things are not working, change is your friend. Perhaps the Top Gun manager with the best finance department can spend a couple of days in your department and give you a leg up. Don't be too proud to ask.

Excellence may not come easy, but the prize is worth the effort. Think about what the states could do with a little work and cooperation. If state income tax must be collected, can we simplify the process to a single sheet of paper? Can we give the taxpayers a break? Is there a way to streamline the automobile licensing process? What can be done about college enrollment and real estate assessment?

I had a long discussion with my state senator in 1965 when Arkansas was debating an automobile inspection law. I tried to explain that inspections are just a farce and the best way to remove dangerous vehicles from the highways is through enforcement. Just because a headlight is burning during an inspection does not mean it will be burning in one month, or in ten minutes for that matter. My plea fell on deaf ears and the law was passed. For the next few decades the taxpayers were subjected to yet another hassle. Trying to get an inspection was like pulling teeth. The inspector was sick or gone to lunch. They were out of inspection stickers. Even brand new cars that had passed a dealership's 50 point inspection had to be inspected. Some inspectors didn't even lay eyes on the automobile and if your horn didn't work, you knew where to find these "friendly" inspectors. Finally, after millions of hours in wasted time, Arkansas did away with automobile inspections. All states can adopt this excellent idea, just say "NO" to inspections and "YES" to law enforcement.

Most states have at least one department or commission that does absolutely nothing but consume tax dollars. Some states don't have such a department. Maybe you can adopt that state's excellence and abolish your "do nothing" department or consolidate. Never be ashamed to probe other programs, organization or companies and adopt the best.

When I was an Operations Group Commander responsible for the squadrons that make up a war machine, an Eighth Air Force Inspector came to fly with us. New inspectors often chose my unit for checkout in our model of the F-16 and seasoned inspectors often chose us for recurrency training. Aside in my office, I explained to the inspector how we continually strived to be the best at what we did. Since I knew the inspector had flown with many units, I asked for his input on how we could improve in some areas. He responded that he had indeed flown with a lot of units and every model of the F-16. He flew with Regular Air Force units, Air Force Reserve Units, Air National Guard Units and even Allied Units. Then he paused and said, "Colonel, there is one unit that is head and shoulders above all the other units, and that is this unit." This inspector had nothing to gain by flattery. We continued to find ways to improve. That is what Top Gun Management is all about.

Have the courage to dream and look forward. You can't move forward if you are always looking back. You can't find new solutions if you believe "it can't be done." Dare to pursue your convictions and reach for the stars. Aristotle was one of the greatest and most influential thinkers in Western culture and probably the most scholarly and learned of the classical Greek philosophers. He was the teacher of Alexander the Great. Aristotle wrote, "We are what we repeatedly do. Excellence, then, is not an act, but a habit." You can choose to be a loser or a winner. It is the Apostle Paul who wrote, "Do you not know that those who run in a race all run, but only one receives the prize? Run in such a way that you may win."

Top Gun Management Principle Number Twelve: Strive for Superiority in all Interactions.

Some huge companies owe much of their success to great customer service. Pleasing customers has been taken to new heights in recent years. This is an area with NO middle ground: you either walk the talk or you don't. If you don't, you stick out like a sore thumb. This will be the longest chapter in the book, mainly because it includes several examples that I believe are necessary to drive home a very key point. Top Gun managers understand that Customer Service is Essential.

Walk-In Medical Clinic in Minnesota

Recently I grew weary of a prolonged heat wave and decided to seek the cool temperatures along the north shore of Lake Superior. On the way I developed an infection and sought advice from my daughter. She told me to go to a walk-in clinic where I could be easily treated with antibiotics. The desk clerk at my hotel informed me that a walk-in clinic at Saint Luke's Hospital was nearby. In a few minutes I was walking into Saint Luke's with low expectations. I expected the usual routine involving a request for identification and proof of insurance followed by the required completion of a multi-page form onto which I would divulge my life history. Many hospitals still pass around a clipboard with the form attached. Imagine the implications of passing a clipboard from one sick person to another. After this ancient routine, I would wait for an hour or more to see a nurse.

You can't blame me for having low expectations after my experiences with military and civilian hospitals for sixty years. Generally, cattle receive more customer-oriented treatment from veterinarians. At least when airlines overbook, they offer you a perk. Clinics and hospitals overbook as a matter of convenience, not for the customer but for themselves. When someone makes an appointment to see me, I honor the appointment unless a dire emergency occurs. It makes no difference if the appointment is with my newest employee or with a visiting dignitary.

But I digress. Back at Saint Luke's Hospital, I actually found a parking space near the entrance. I was impressed, a parking space for a customer -- what a novel idea. I walked up to the counter and told them I needed to see a doctor. I was immediately taken to a private room where a nurse quickly interviewed me regarding my symptoms. I was then promptly shown to an examination room where fluid specimens were obtained. Following this, a young lady entered the room and entered some of my demographic information (name, address, medications, and allergies) into a computer terminal. Simultaneously, a physician's assistant checked my vital signs. The doctor then entered the room with the results of my tests and wrote a prescription for me. He said the drugs would help me feel better soon and that I should check with my doctor in a month or so to rule out any other possible problem. Some cases require a second round of antibiotics. The *last* order of business on my visit to Saint Luke's was the inquiry about health insurance. A move to Duluth simply to have access to such a hospital is tempting.

The entire time spent inside Saint Luke's Hospital was much shorter than the time I am accustomed to waiting before even talking to any hospital or clinic staff member. Many years ago, my wife severed the tip of her finger. As you can imagine, such an injury is very painful and quite bloody. To this day, she talks about awaiting treatment in the waiting room for over an hour and a half.

Fortunately, she was a Registered Nurse on maternity leave at the time and had disinfected the injury before leaving home.

A good friend of mine went to another Minnesota clinic for an evaluation. He told me he walked into the Mayo Clinic and picked up a magazine on the way to the counter. He walked out of the clinic after the evaluation never having had time to open the magazine.

I see a direct correlation between customer oriented medical care and life expectancy. Minnesota has the second highest life expectancy in the nation slightly less than Hawaii. My home state of Arkansas ranks 44th and is one of three states without a trauma bill linking hospitals to help patients who suffer traumatic injuries.

Males born in the nation's capitol have the lowest life expectancy at 68 ½ years. Infant mortality rate is also highest in Washington, DC. Are we more concerned about saving the northern spotted owl than saving human lives? Are more efforts going into preventing oil drilling in the Arctic National Wildlife Refuge than into improving human health care?

Minnesota is not the only state with great customer-oriented clinics and hospitals, but these two examples tower in my mind as the embodiment of what can be achieved by truly pursuing excellence.

The United States Postal Service

After highlighting what I believe is superiority in interactions at Saint Luke's Hospital, I will now explore the far end of the spectrum: the United States Postal Service. In years past, a sense of pride was easily detectable in their mantra:

"Neither snow nor rain nor heat nor gloom of night stays these couriers from the swift completion of their appointed rounds."

In truth, this has never been the official motto of the United States Postal Service. The inscription was supplied by William Mitchell Kendall of the architecture firm McKim, Mead & White, who designed the New York General Post Office. According to Kendall, the sentence appears in the works of Herodotus and describes the expedition of the Greeks against the Persians under Cyrus, about 500 B.C. The Persians operated a system of mounted postal couriers, and the sentence describes the fidelity with which their work was accomplished.

The Postal Reorganization Act of 1970 abolished the United States Post Office Department of the cabinet and created the United States Postal Service, a corporation-like independent agency with an official monopoly on the delivery of mail in the United States. The USPS is the third-largest employer in the United

States, falling just behind the United States Department of Defense and Wal-Mart. The post office operates the largest civilian vehicle fleet in the world, with an estimated 260,000 vehicles.

What does this independent agency do for me? Remember when there seemed to be a blue mailbox on almost every intersection in America? They are gone. Better to make you and me drive around endlessly looking for a post office than to bother with customer-oriented convenience. I often find the few mailboxes outside post offices to be completely full. People stuff letters and padded envelopes in the box as best they can with the hope that they won't get rained on or blow away. You can mail a letter in a box at one post office and it will be picked up at 11 AM that day; but several blocks away, your mail may sit for over 48 hours before retrieval by the postal service.

The USPS holds a statutory monopoly on non-urgent First Class Mail, outbound U.S. international letters as well as the exclusive right to put mail in private mailboxes, as described in the Private Express Statutes. In other words, the mailboxes that you and I purchase and install are not available to our relatives, neighbors or any of the post office's competitors. The law that prohibits anyone except the USPS from placing mail in a private mailbox (18 U.S.C. § 1725), was passed for two reasons: preventing loss of revenue to the post office and "to decrease the quantity of extraneous matter being placed in mail boxes."

Well, that certainly worked! Do you note any drop in extraneous junk mail? In spite of all the protection and subsidies and perks provided to the USPS, the competition is flourishing delivering the overnight letters and parcels allowed. In fact, FedEx and others have captured 90% of the overnight mail business. Can it be because they do it better and at lower rates?

Multiple attempts at starting independent non-government subsidized mail delivery companies have been made by entrepreneurs dating back to the 1830's. These included Lysander Spooner and his American Letter Mail Company, Henry Wells of Wells Fargo, Alvin Adams and the Pony Express. They were all eventually forced out of business through Congressional legislation, allowing the US Postal Service to maintain its monopoly on mail delivery. This has been to the criticism of many, including Nobel Prize winning economist Milton Friedman and Jim Kelly of UPS. More and more, the defects of the Postal Service stand in contrast to the successes of the private sector created services that are part of the telecommunications revolution.

I ship a lot of items as an eBay Power Seller. The USPS regulations boggle the mind. Some items must be over ¾ inches thick to be mailed, others must be less than ¼ inch. Even postal clerks cannot keep up with all the regulations, and rather than argue with a clerk who claims my parcel does not meet standards, I simply go to a different post office. For the reader with strong intestinal fortitude, take a moment to read Appendix A: Postal Code Changes which provides a glimpse into the convoluted world of USPS regulations.

There is a Postal Watch organization that keeps watch over the postal service, but in light of my own experiences, I will forgo the horror stories of others.

Recently, I attempted to ship a package to Canada but was unable to connect to the USPS website that allows me to purchase and print shipping labels. I printed an address label and filled out a custom form for shipment by Letter Post. Upon arrival at a local post office I joined a waiting line extending from the only open station out of the counter area, through a door and into the lobby. When the counter was finally in sight, I noticed a second clerk preparing to open another station. I finally reached the counter and was informed that I could not send the package by Letter Post and the customs form I had filled out was the wrong form. I was given several other expensive options. Perhaps it was my grimace that prompted the clerk to recheck and determine that I could, in fact, use Letter Post and I had filled out the correct customs form after all. I left before the other clerk ever managed to open the second station.

Currently you can ship a one ounce item by First Class Mail. The cost is $0.312, $0.334, $0.341, $0.360, $0.373, $0.41, $0.80 or $1.13. Actually there are even more options for discounted flats, etc. More than half of the USPS revenue comes from First Class, approximately $37 billion per year. That is down from previous years, I wonder why.

I should hasten to say that I rank one federal entity far below the USPS. That would be the Inspector General system (IG). Every department has an IG with a staff of investigators. Every military base has one. They are a government watchdog, designed to police fraud, waste and abuse. Based on what I have seen, the system is badly broken, costing the taxpayers billions of dollars a year.

Government waste is legendary. Yet government employees know that if they report the waste they observe, their career will be damaged. The focus of the ensuing IG investigation will likely be the person who reported the fraud, waste or abuse instead of the entity reported. Allegations are rarely substantiated.

The IG is not independently functioning and may actually work for the accused party. If the IG finds and substantiates fraud it could make the agency look bad.

Victims are rarely permitted to seek redress in the courts. The only justice available to government whistleblowers, in my opinion, comes from the courts if they are granted the permission to sue after the IG fails to substantiate the allegations. For these reasons, I think the largest fraud, waste and abuse is committed by the IGs themselves.

Generals, admirals and department heads always seem to want the biggest and most expensive. That is why we have two billion dollar airplanes and submarines while combat personnel went to war without body armor or armored vehicles. Until we have an independent agency investigating fraud, waste and abuse, similar to the Government Accountability Office, America will continue to spend billions and billions of dollars indiscriminately.

"Service" Stations

I still remember when I could pull into a service station and stay in my car. The attendant would fill up my tank with gasoline, wash my windshield, check my oil and tire pressure and then receive my payment. While most businesses were embracing Doctor Deming's methods of

Total Quality Management focusing on customer service and embracing a strategy aimed at embedding awareness of quality in all organizational processes, service stations evolved into gas stations. Service vanished in favor of disservice. Customers now must pay in advance which means two trips inside unless "pay at the pump" is available. In many cases you must even pay for air. Yet, society has seemed to accept this, probably because most people have been infected by a virus of disempowerment that tells them "you can't change anything, so you might as well accept things the way they are" … but that's an entirely different topic.

I submit that Top Gun managers understand the importance of quality interactions and true respect for others. Whether they strike a target deep inside enemy territory within seconds of the assigned time over target or they arrive at a meeting on time and prepared, they perform as professionals. They are considerate and respect others. Yes, they use their turn signals and use the passing lane for passing. They walk on the right side of the hallway or sidewalk instead of making others get out of their way. Rudeness and self-centered behavior has no place in the Top Gun Universe and The Golden Rule still applies today just as it did two thousand years ago.

Top Gun Management Principle Number Thirteen: Exhaust Your Resources.

One summer when I was about thirteen I helped my neighbor, Mister Parks, haul hay. It was an honor to be able to help out on the large farm he owned. The dried hay had been raked and now needed to be picked up with pitchforks and placed on a wagon. Once the hay had been stacked high on the wagon, we could head for the barn. Once in the barn, Mr. Parks had a device that would plunge into the hay, then secure the load with two prongs. After that, the hay would be hoisted up and locked on a pulley, then travel to the back of the loft while hanging from a rail.

My job involved moving the hay to the back of the barn and releasing it with a jerk of the release cord. The hot sun beating down on the tin roof of the barn made the temperature inside the loft similar to an oven. Dust and pieces of hay drifted down inside the back of my shirt. This was my introduction to farm work.

I was especially hot, tired and sweaty one day and suggested to Mr. Parks it might be nice to get some more help. The wisdom he imparted to me has remained with me all my life. In fact, I repeated what he told me at the state conference of the Farm Bureau while on the gubernatorial campaign trail. Mr. Parks said, "One boy will do the work of one boy. Two boys will do the work of half a boy and three boys will not do any work at all." I told the delegates that our state was approaching the three boy limit and needed to be streamlined and downsized.

Late in my career, I once had about one hundred thousand dollars in my civilian pay budget that I did not need. It could have been used to hire temporary or fulltime personnel, or moved to another account and used to buy furniture or motivational pictures. Members of my staff wanted to hire temporary employees to do their work. I did not want to hire people to do their work, I wanted my employees to do their own work. I turned the money back to the government. It was given to another director who also didn't need it.

I know that some receive an ego boost from managing a huge budget. Others fear that without a large budget, they might actually have to manage rather than throw excess money at projects. I have heard of sailors dumping food and supplies into the ocean on their return to port for fear that supplies would be cut on future deployments. A real Top Gun manager makes wise use of resources and cuts out waste at every opportunity. Top Gun managers are rare.

Setting goals is an important way to maximize your resources. Goals you set for yourself, or others, should be SMART: Specific, Measurable, Achievable, Realistic, and have a specific Timeline.

F-100s from the Arkansas Air National Guard refueling from an Air Force KC-135

Chapter Eight:

Fatal Management Blunders

Some people in leadership positions have serious misconceptions about their role as part of the working team. I hope to dispel some of these misconceptions and highlight several common blunders with the hope that you will avoid them.

Top Gun Management Principle Number Fourteen: Leave Public Relations to Public Relations.

Someone in your organization is responsible for public relations (some call it media relations or public affairs, but it's all the same). Most likely, that person is not you. People in public relations generally have something called a Public Relations degree and know how to do their job better than you. It is your responsibility, however, to keep them informed.

I have known top executives who think their job is public relations. They would much rather smile in front of a TV camera than to make the tough decisions required to lead their company. They love showing the school kids around the plant and explaining the intricacies of production. I still recall when Wal-Mart CEO David Glass publicly defended their "Buy America" program. Earning public understanding and acceptance can be a slippery slope for a top executive. Many still remember when Secretary of State Alexander Hague announced that he was in charge following the attempted assassination of President Reagan. Had he read the Presidential Succession Act of 1947, however, he would have known that the Secretary of State falls behind the Vice President, the Speaker of the House, and the President pro tempore of the Senate. Today, most Presidents leave public announcements to the Press Secretary.

Why the boss loves to do public relations work but eschews janitor work is not hard to understand. Take your foot out of your mouth and heed the principle and sage advice given. Make the tough decisions, do your job and earn your paycheck while leaving PR work to the professionals.

Top Gun Management Principle Number Fifteen: Abolish All Unnecessary Meetings.

I once called the Adjutant General and was informed by his assistant that he was in a meeting with the Governor. I told them I I wanted to talk to the adjutant general right then. They interrupted the meeting and he took my call.

"What's up?" he asked.

I told him an F-4 had just crashed. The AG asked what he could do to help. I requested two helicopters. He said he would send them immediately and then asked what he should tell the press. I asked him not to say anything yet, but assured him I would contact him with an update. We took care of an important matter in a few short minutes and he resumed his meeting with the Governor.

How many times have you heard "Mr. or Mrs. So-and-So is in a meeting right now, can I take a message?" Some of my division chiefs loved meetings. When calling them, I was frequently told they were in a meeting. That never stopped me from talking to them, but it did insulate them from most everyone else.

With local area networks, cell phones and

Blackberries™, email and instant messaging, most formal meetings should become obsolete. I recall when my organization had a command and control meeting every morning. We would first sit through a briefing on the status of the jets, the flying schedule, the weather, the parts and supply status and so forth. Then we would go around the table listening to what each director thought was important. The whole thing usually took almost an hour. That information could have easily been placed on the department intranet. If a particular division had issues, they could have met without wasting everyone else's time.

Too often meetings provide forums for individuals to impress others with their importance. Rarely does anything of substance emerge and almost never is anything solved. The guy who sits at the head of the table may get an ego boost from all the power and others may be happy to have a seat at the table rather than having to work. Meetings present an illusion of efficiency and organization while wasting an enormous amount of time. In the words of the comedian Milton Berle, "A committee is a group that keeps minutes and loses hours."

Don't misunderstand me here. Some meetings are productive and necessary, especially if your executives don't otherwise talk to each other. But if they are not communicating despite the presence of meetings, there are bigger problems at hand.

Abolish all meetings that are not absolutely necessary. If you must hold meetings, have an agenda and keep focused. Don't allow rabbit chasing and don't invite people who are not absolutely essential to achieving the objective.

The great economist John Kenneth Galbraith (1908–2006) was a prolific author who taught at Harvard University for many years. Galbraith was active in politics, serving in the administrations of Franklin D. Roosevelt, Harry S. Truman, John F. Kennedy and Lyndon B. Johnson; and among other roles served as U.S. ambassador to India under Kennedy. He was one of very few two-time recipients of the Presidential Medal of Freedom. He received one from President Truman in 1946 and another from President Bill Clinton in 2000. He was also awarded the Padma Vibhushan, India's second highest civilian award, for his contributions to strengthening ties between India and the United States. John Kenneth Galbraith had this to say, "Meetings are indispensable when you don't want to do anything."

Top Gun Management Principle Number Sixteen: Never Practice or Tolerate Discrimination in Any Form.

Late in my career, I needed to hire a new assistant. This person would not only function as my administrative assistant but would also serve as the quality control officer. It was a mid-level federal position and we advertised nationwide. The human resource office delivered about 10 applications which they had certified as qualified. In the end, I hired a person who was working for the US Department of Justice and had traveled about 1,000 miles for the interview. She happened to be a black female. I was not aware of any racial prejudices in my organization and never hesitated to hire minorities, my former secretary being another black female who obtained a bachelor's degree in night school before obtaining a commission in the Air Force and moving away. Perhaps I had been naïve, because I soon heard that a senior official had made a statement to the effect that "Colonel McVay hires blacks whether they are qualified or not."

Was the specter of racial discrimination and bigotry raising its ugly head? The person I had hired made a lateral move from a similar position with the Justice Department: she had a master's degree and was working toward a PhD. Not surprisingly, shortly after I retired she accepted a higher position in the Washington, DC area and moved. We still communicate.

I don't recall God asking me what race I wanted to be or where I would like to be born. I might have chosen to be born with a silver spoon in my mouth into the House of Windsor. Or perhaps I might have chosen to be a Rockefeller, Getty or Rothschild. The fact is we don't choose our circumstances. I will never understand how anyone can be ignorant enough to believe they are somehow better than someone else because of the color of their skin. Why some Southerners hate Northerners and vice versa, why fat people hate skinny people or why some hate people because of the color of their hair are concepts I abhor and cannot understand. To express hatred and bitterness toward people merely because they are different is inherently wrong and especially repugnant.

One would think that by 2007 Americans would have moved far beyond racial hatred and discrimination, but alas they have not. It still lurks below the surface. If you are afflicted please give this book to someone else because you are not worthy to even consider becoming a Top Gun manager.

Top Gun Management Principle Number Seventeen: Never Abuse Your Power.

I obtained a university minor in history many years ago, yet I only developed a passion for history in later life. I love ancient history, world history, colonial history, and the history of the United States as well as Bible history. When researching Egyptian history I chose to use a text ignored by most Egyptologists: the Holy Bible. The Bible tells the story of Joseph who was sold into bondage by his brothers and rose to become second in power only to the pharaoh. Joseph saved Egypt and most of the rest of the known world from a seven year famine. When you save the lives of millions of people, you become a great hero in the eyes of the people.

There are two prominent items in the royal regalia of ancient Egypt that particularly interest me, the crook (heka) and the flail or flabellum (nekhakha). While I can't substantiate this anywhere, I believe they were used by the pharaoh in his or her capacity as judge. I think the pharaoh listened to the accused and the accuser and rendered a judgment without speaking. If the accused was deemed innocent, the Shepherd's crook was raised. If judged guilty, the flail was raised. The way pharaoh held the flail determined the degree of punishment. Pharaoh held the power of life or death over his subjects.

Like that pharaoh of long ago, top managers today often serve as judges. In many instances, if your employee does not receive justice from you, he or she will probably not receive justice at all. With that great authority comes great responsibility. The discipline process must be deliberate, fair and even-handed. Employees should not be punished for honest mistakes. The punishment must fit the offense. Like in a properly functioning justice system, the employee is innocent until proven guilty. Never be cavalier as you mete out punishment, remembering that your actions may have far reaching consequences and affect many other people including family members. Never take action when you are angry (this may require counting to more than 10 or 100) and never repay evil with evil.

I remember a scenario in my younger days when a certain man in my town had enormous power. He once told a business owner that if a certain person worked for him, he would have to let him go. That person was subsequently fired without reason. I always believed that the fired person had simply not paid sufficient deference or reverence toward the big shot living in his ivory tower of the 1960s.

The days have mostly passed when one person can

brandish so much power that they can blackball someone from the workforce in a whole town. Nevertheless, employers have taken firing to new heights of unfairness. If an employee is too involved in union activities, management will find another reason to let them go. Top Gun managers play fair and do not participate in such underhanded schemes.

Chapter Nine:

Vital Management Qualities

Top Gun Management Principle Number Eighteen: Develop Courage.

Two and a quarter centuries ago, a new flag emerged. It was seen in battle during the Revolutionary War. The new flag was first raised above a ship by Captain John Paul Jones. The flag was seen in the Atlantic and the Pacific and in foreign ports. In May of 1812 the United States Flag was hoisted above the Catamount Schoolhouse in Colrain, Massachusetts marking the first time the Stars and Strips had ever flown over a public school. Today the flag flies above thousands of schoolhouses in America and at embassy and armed forces schools around the world. Our Flag has even flown above the surface of the Moon.

Old Glory represents you and me, our country, the American way of life and our government, and around the world our Flag represents Freedom.

The color red in the Stars and Strips represents "Courage." You may be familiar with this concept. You may think that courage only applies to combat solders and SWAT teams. The word courage derives from the French word for *coeur*, meaning heart. Courage is the ability to stand by one's heart or to stand by one's core. **Courage is the very essence of leadership and management**. Courage is as fundamental to good leadership as a scalpel is to a good surgeon.

It took courage for Frederick W. Smith to start a company in Little Rock, Arkansas in 1971 called Federal Express. Fred Smith was from Mississippi and graduated from Yale as a classmate of George Bush. He then served his country for five years in the United States Marine Corps. Smith had the courage to start the business, but Little Rock Airport Authorities would not agree to provide facilities. Smith found that he was welcome in Memphis, Tennessee where FedEx began its climb into the List of Fortune 500 Companies. It ranked 70 on this list in 2006, employing close to 200,000 people. One of the largest customers of FedEx is the United States Postal Service.

Courage should not be confused with fearlessness

or being unafraid. Courage is the willingness to do your duty in spite of fear. Courage may not take the form of audacious heroism. Sometimes just making a decision takes courage. We have all dealt with indecisive people, that boss who must have reams of information only to find excuse after painful excuse to avoid making a critical decision.

Too many managers choose caution and inaction. They are afraid of appearing either too conservative or too radical. They stand out as passionless, mediocre, and unmemorable. The answer to "What will people think?" is that they will think nothing. It's a courageous act to take a stand. We develop courage by facing our fears and tackling the big problems and questions. When we label fear as bad or something to avoid, we create resistance that can disproportionately magnify it. Our unconscious suppression numbs and deadens us and keeps us from living life fully in the moment.

When we seek excellence over perfection, authenticity is unveiled. Sometimes we make the mistake of equating vulnerability with softness or weakness. Yet the truth is that we all have a sensitive core. Strength is not petrified hardness but mental and emotional agility. When we're in conflict emotionally, our bodies are twisted. When we let go of the facade, it shows up in our eyes and our voices. Sharing our uniqueness conveys how special we are. When we admit our vulnerabilities, we expose our true selves – without apology.

It was the great visionary Walt Disney who said, "All our dreams can come true – if we have the courage to pursue them." Top Gun managers are not stymied by fear of making a mistake or appearing foolish. They courageously give themselves full permission to take chances and make mistakes. Willingness to fail or make a mistake has a power all its own. Far less is learned from doing things right than learning from failure. Many entrepreneurs have admitted that their early failures and bankruptcies taught more than any university degree.

Winston Churchill was the British Prime Minister and Minister of Defense during World War II. Sir Winston Leonard Spencer-Churchill was one of the most important leaders in modern British and world history. He won the 1953 Nobel Prize in Literature for his many books on English and world history. He was voted the greatest-ever Briton in the 2002 BBC poll the 100 Greatest Britons. Churchill's greatest achievement was that he refused to capitulate when defeat by Germany was a strong possibility; instead, he remained a strong opponent of any negotiations with Germany. Few others in the Cabinet had this degree of resolve. By adopting this policy, Churchill maintained Britain as a base from which the Allies could attack Germany, thereby ensuring that the Soviet sphere of influence did not extend over Western Europe at the end of the war.

Churchill displayed a high degree of courage during the most tumultuous and dangerous period of world history. On the subject he said, "Courage is rightly considered the foremost of the virtues, for upon it, all others depend."

Top Gun Management Principle Number Nineteen: Overcome Adversity:

If you just received a fatal wound or were diagnosed with a fatal illness, you are facing adversity. Otherwise you are probably just being hassled. Most of us have not yet achieved perfection and therefore face trials and adversity on a daily basis. While we may not be able to control events, we *can* control how we react or overreact to them. Adversity can be natural or manmade, an inconvenience or a catastrophe.

Few have faced as much adversity as Mother Teresa during her ministry to the poverty-stricken people of Calcutta. The Nobel Peace Prize recipient said, "I know God will not give me anything I can't handle. I just wish that He didn't trust me so much."

I recall when I received my third stripe in the Air Force. I had one year and nine months in the service at the time. I noticed after I sewed on the stripes I faced adversity daily. I was sent to clean the latrines while those of lesser rank sat idle. Even though we had janitors, I was assigned to mop and empty trash. When President Kennedy was assassinated, I was ordered to guard a generator outside the cantonment area in four feet of snow. I noticed I was not receiving equal treatment. I noticed but never complained. I took whatever they gave me.

One day the commander and superintendent called me into the office. They asked me if I had noticed that I was on the top of the list for every dirty detail. I told them I had noticed. They then told me that they were testing my fabric and character and I had passed. As of that date, I would be off all details and was being assigned to the position of Assistant Analysis and Reporting Controller. What a huge and exciting responsibility for a twenty year old kid! It would be many years before I would ever have as much responsibility again.

It was the founder of Ford Motor Company, Henry Ford, who said, "Life is a series of experiences, each one of which makes us bigger, even though sometimes it is hard to realize this. For the world was built to develop character, and we must learn that the setbacks and grief's which we endure help us in our marching onward."

I just happen to be wearing a T-shirt that reads, "That which does not kill me only makes me stronger." The shirt was a gift from my daughter that she bought while attending Air Force Officer Training. The quote is not attributed, but comes from the German-Swiss philosopher and writer, Friedrich Nietzsche (1844-1900).

The challenge of overcoming hard times tempers our spirit and deepens our resolve. "Adversity has the effect of eliciting talents which in prosperous circumstances would have lain dormant." – Horace (B.C. 68-65)

Those above you and those below you will carefully watch how you deal with adversity. Will you, like Nero, fiddle while Rome burns or react like David Glasgow Farragut? Flag Officer Farragut was onboard his flag ship the USS Hartford when he shouted his famous order during the Civil War Battle of Mobile Bay, "Damn the torpedoes, full speed ahead!" He was not talking about submarine torpedoes. In those days, tethered naval mines were known as torpedoes and they had already destroyed one of his ships. Farragut's reaction to adversity gave him victory. The United States showed its appreciation by promoting him to Rear Admiral. He holds the distinction of being the Navy's first Rear Admiral, Vice Admiral and Full Admiral. His quote took its place in history alongside great quotes like, "Veni, Vedi, Vici (I came, I saw, I conquered)" by Julius Caesar and, "I have not yet begun to fight!" by John Paul Jones.

We must accept adversity and learn from it so that over time we will gain the experience to properly deal with it. If we react to problems like an ostrich, they won't go away. Believe me; countless managers try to ignore adversity. Things don't get better of their own accord, they get worse. Before you can attack a problem, you have to accept the fact that there is a problem (See Principle #4).

Top Gun Principle Number Twenty: Foster Optimism and a Can-Do Attitude.

Winston Churchill said, "I am an optimist. It does not seem too much use being anything else."

Optimism and enthusiasm can become infectious. As a factor in success and personal growth and development, optimism cannot be over estimated. Optimism gives you the power to capitalize on each and every possibility. Ideas and inventions do not come from negativity and despair. It is optimism that is responsible for success in most aspects of life. I am absolutely convinced that optimism results in higher achievement and greater excellence.

By being optimistic, I am not suggesting that you look at the world through rose-colored glasses or become frivolous. I am suggesting that optimism physically activates a very important portion of your brain that increases your ability to create constructive answers to real challenges.

You undoubtedly know someone who is consistently negative, having no ability to see available options when situations go askew. Complaining is a symptom of this kind of thinking. Is the glass half full or half empty? A positive outlook tends to expand your ability to achieve, to learn, and to accomplish. A sincere belief in yourself and your capability to positively impact your circumstances fosters excellence and success.

I believe there is always something to look forward to if you gently move your mind into positive, optimistic thoughts whenever you find yourself feeling negative, dejected, or wallowing in despair. The rainbow is there and the clouds have silver linings. If you look, you will see them. Let these quotes inspire you:

> Even if I knew that tomorrow the world would go to pieces, I would still plant my apple tree. – Martin Luther

> No pessimist ever discovered the secrets of the stars, or sailed to an uncharted land, or opened a new heaven to the human spirit.
> – Helen Keller

If you fall into the despondent pit, you will undoubtedly take your employees with you – and your organization will suffer.

Closing Thoughts

I want to leave you with a model of a life lived in excellence – one that demonstrates the key points of what I want you to glean from this book. Someone who did it right: George Washington Carver.

He taught himself to read. His family was so poverty-stricken; he couldn't afford to buy a new pencil; so he made a holder and used a pencil that was only ¼ inch long. He wanted to get an education. When he was 12 years old, he left home to attend a black school. There was only one teacher in a small room filled with 75 children. While other children played at recess, he studied. He studied at home before and after he did his chores. Soon he knew more than his teacher. He wrote to a college requesting enrollment and they accepted him, but changed their minds when they found out he was black.

After five more years, when he was 30 years old, he was accepted to a college in Iowa. He flourished, and his teacher helped him transfer to Iowa State College where he studied botany. He learned about plants and farming. He became the top botany student on campus.

Young Carver did many things to earn and save money to pay for his expenses including selling hominy which he had made and sometimes ironing clothes for his classmates. He found an old stove at the city dump and brought it home to cook meals for his friends. He used old wrapping paper for notebooks. "Don't throw anything away," he would say. "Everything can be used again."

After graduation, the college invited him to stay and teach biology to new students. He was later asked to teach at the Tuskegee Institute in Alabama.

Carver started studying diseases that were attacking the farmers' crops. He also did a lot of experimenting to find new ways to use different plants. He made more than 300 products from peanuts – even soap and ink. From sweet potatoes, he made 118 products, including flour and candy. He made 75 products from pecans and even used cotton stalks to create a building material for walls. He had many novel ideas!

Later in life, Thomas Edison offered him $100,000 a year to be in his employment. That would be about two million dollars a year in today's money. Carver declined, believing he would be of more benefit at Tuskegee.

He made his students work hard and insisted they do each experiment right. If they told him they had done something "about right," he would say, "Don't tell me it's 'about right.' If it's 'about right,' then it's wrong."

Money, stylish clothes, and fine cars were not important to him. He thought the truly successful person was the one who had learned to serve others.

He was one of the finest scientists the world has ever known.

***

As you reach the final page of this book, it is my hope that you have moved inexorably toward your goal of becoming the Best of the Best. When the race is over it is important to maintain your respect for yourself. You must be able to look yourself in the eye and you must like who you see. Along the way perhaps you will have the courage to reach for the stars.

Appendix A

Postal Code Changes

The definition of the current nonstandard surcharge will be expanded to include certain physical criteria that could make a mailpiece nonmachinable. Pieces that are nonmachinable are excluded from automated processing and must be handled manually. Nonmachinable pieces also may impede mail flow or damage the mail or mail processing equipment. Manual pieces are considerably more costly to process than machinable letters.

The criteria for nonmachinable letter–size pieces will be listed in DMM C050.2.2. The nonmachinable surcharge will apply to single–piece and Presorted rate letters that weigh 1 ounce or less and meet one or more of the criteria in that section. Machinable pieces are not subject to any restrictions regarding the OCR read area or barcode clear zone.

The nonmachinable surcharge also will apply to single–piece, Presorted, and automation rate nonletters (flats and parcels) that weigh 1 ounce or less if any one of the following applies:

(a) The piece is greater than 1/4–inch thick.

(b) The length is more than 11–1/2 inches or the height is more than 6–1/8 inches.

(c) The aspect ratio (length divided by height) is less than 1.3 or more than 2.5.

The nonmachinable surcharge will be $0.12 for single–piece rate pieces and $0.055 for Presorted and automation rate pieces.

The nonmachinable criteria in C050.2.2 do not apply to pieces mailed at any card rate.

The nonmachinable surcharge will apply to letter–size pieces (but not card–rate pieces) for which the mailer has chosen the manual only (do not automate) option. For card–rate pieces, a mailer can specify manual handling, but they will not be charged a surcharge.

This change is consistent with the addition of a nonmachinable surcharge for Standard Mail service.

In conjunction with this change, trays of

machinable and nonmachinable letters will be prepared and labeled differently. The preparation for machinable letters will be similar to the current preparation for upgradable letters (e.g., no packaging, optional 5–digit sort level); the preparation for nonmachinable pieces will be similar to the current package–based preparation for Presorted letters. The current weight limit for upgradable letters (2.5 ounces) will be replaced with a weight limit of 3.3 ounces for machinable letters. Letters heavier than 3.3 ounces and less than 1/4–inch thick will use the nonmachinable preparation and labeling but will not pay the surcharge (because it applies only to pieces that weigh 1 ounce or less).

On tray labels, the current "NON BC" (not barcoded) designation will be replaced with one of two designations: "MACH" for machinable pieces or "MANUAL" for nonmachinable pieces. Although card–rate pieces will not be subject to the surcharge, mailers will be required to show on the tray label whether or not those pieces are machinable (for instance, a double card that is not tabbed is not machinable). The "MANUAL" designation will help the Postal Service direct trays of mail to the appropriate mail processing operation. As is currently required, mailers who choose the "do not automate" option will show "MANUAL" on Line 2 of the tray label.

Barcoded tray labels are allowed, but are not required, for trays of First–Class Mail machinable letters. Zebra codes must not be used on trays of First–Class Mail machinable letters. (Zebra codes indicate that the tray contains automation rate prebarcoded mail.)

There are no preparation or labeling changes for Presorted flats or parcels subject to the surcharge.

Mail preparation instructions for Presorted letter–size pieces subject to the nonmachinable surcharge will be included in DMM M130. Preparation instructions for automation flats subject to the nonmachinable surcharge will not change (see current DMM M820).

The nonmachinable surcharge will be assessed on any piece mailed out as a different class of mail and returned as a First–Class Mail item (for instance, a Standard Mail item endorsed "Return Service Requested") if the piece weighs 1 ounce or less and meets the criteria for nonmachinability in C050.2.2. Pieces returned at First–Class Mail card rates will not be subject to the nonmachinable surcharge.

The nonmachinable surcharge will take effect when new rates are implemented; however, mailers have until January 1, 2003, to comply with the mail preparation and tray labeling changes.

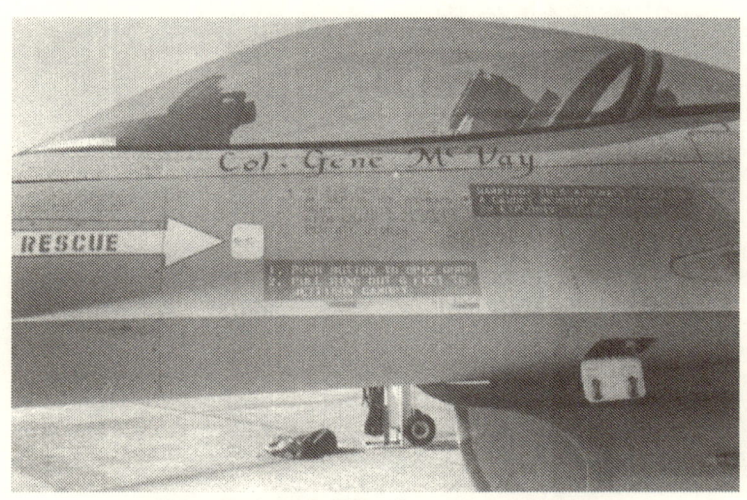

Contact Information

Comments and requests should be sent to the author at the following Email address: genemcvay@aol.com